TIME IS THE ENEMY

Time is the Enemy

Poems
by
MATT BARKER

Adelaide Books
New York / Lisbon
2019

TIME IS THE ENEMY
Poems
By Matt Barker

Copyright © by Matt Barker

Cover design © 2019 Adelaide Books
Cover image by Ariel Tobing

Published by Adelaide Books, New York / Lisbon
adelaidebooks.org

Editor-in-Chief
Stevan V. Nikolic

All rights reserved. No part of this book may be reproduced in any manner whatsoever without written permission from the author except in the case of brief quotations embodied in critical articles and reviews.

For any information, please address Adelaide Books
at info@adelaidebooks.org
or write to:
Adelaide Books
244 Fifth Ave. Suite D27
New York, NY, 10001

ISBN-10: 1-951214-43-9
ISBN-13: 978-1-951214-43-2

Printed in the United States of America

Dedicated to Brett Billings

June 2, 1992 – May 9, 2017

miss you bro

Contents

Deposit *11*

A Product of Force *12*

Agreed Importance *13*

Purge *14*

Missionary *15*

Stray *16*

Graduation *17*

Bad Aim *18*

PSA *19*

Delayed Resumption *20*

Update *21*

Square Up *23*

4:19 AM *24*

25/8   *25*

4-D   *26*

Black Falcon   *29*

Shotgun   *30*

MFA   *32*

Lackluster Overcompensation   *33*

24   *34*

Déjà Vu   *36*

Ode to Brett Billings   *37*

No Mad   *39*

Poem to Rant   *40*

Bad Habit   *41*

Peanut Gallery   *42*

Token   *43*

86'D   *44*

Solid   *45*

Ozzy   *46*

Break   *47*

Competition   *49*

TIME IS THE ENEMY

College Conversations **50**

Mentiroso **51**

Reach **52**

Accounting **53**

Bar Back **54**

Cigarette Contemplation **55**

Rhetoric **56**

Light **58**

Clockwork **59**

Felt Pressure **60**

Polar **61**

Typed **62**

Half Full **63**

About the Author **65**

Deposit

the day is drowning
unable to endure
the unflinching trickle of time

writers never die
effortlessly evading extinction
inevitable immortality implied in ink
molded by the momentary mindset

                it will come

                don't take it

                              too seriously............

A Product of Force

I am not the biggest
fan
of talking

about myself

now please
allow me to digress
into my hypocrisy

I am usually too busy
thinking
about x, y, and z

these words
this poem
have not and never will
complete the ordered objective
aware of their doomed voluntary mission
attendance is sparse

the creator does not pretend
to believe in
his orders

Agreed Importance

the uninitiated surreal tangerines

are not

                         in season

                         as I am

self served

                                        a plate of dried fears

Purge

Recently,

          I have been guilty

          of leaving
          the paper

                    blank

a writer

is only
as good
as the ink

          that makes it
          onto the paper

I am scared

I might have

                    lost it…..

Missionary

a crime of passion
no condom
fitting skeleton key
the
infallible phallus
a product
of the demon's semen

                just

                    skippin stones

                        off rocks

Stray

I am sorry
I hear you but I am not listening

it is off to the races
once again
up in between the ears

I am lost again

                                      running in and out
                                      of this and that

occasionally
you will not even be registered

I wonder

why now
x, y, and z
will not be denied

                  front and center

I wonder
if I can get

                  out

              diagnosed detrimental cathartic creativity
                                  cannot be aborted

Graduation

        a man

        rich

        in regrets

cannot lose

        the past

Bad Aim

heavy breaths
summon
the slow roll
of liquid
the non-negotiable swell
conducts
heavy foam filled seas
are
putting on weight
sip by sip
throwing themselves
upon
soft fleshy levees
fueling
my panicked porcelain prance

fuck

I pissed on the seat

PSA

the mortal witness
in their corruptible body
must be headstrong
for it to remain
attached
the exterminator is cuming
onto the menace of society
when the pigs no longer protect
it is
every animal for themself

Delayed Resumption

immortal ink
ever
withstanding words

souvenirs
of the dead man

                I quite like
                this idea

                              I really need
                              to produce more

                                                products…

Update

the modern day
will less warrior
suffers
wi-fi wanderlust withdrawals
hiding beneath
layers of name brands
forging artificial armor
creating commercialized courage
veterans fight
a losing battle
against anti-social media
with
the ever present
electronic leash
deep seeded
within our span
yanking us back
to virtual unreality
with a mindless addictive click
the refresh button is targeted

Matt Barker

our imagination, dreams, wandering thoughts

are kept

within

arms reach

step away

from the screens

create a connection

Square Up

drowned empty
lifeless words
wash my ears
not a trace
left behind

                              this map
                              of math
                              is useless
                              leading me
                              further astray
                              deeper
                              into
                              this cigarette ashtray

4:19 AM

to the beat
of
single sporadic
taps
ambitious ashes
begin their
final dance

enjoying

their time
before
the inevitable
inverted
fall

upon arrival
the itinerary
constantly consists
of being
stepped on
and
forgotten

25/8

robotic movements
set the mood
I am emotionless
foreplay forgotten
as I begin
to strip
my mind
in search of
spiritual sensuality
I came
to appreciate
this same old song
that never gets old
when you
are
courting creativity

4-D

that one time
waiting
for my fungal growth
to blossom
I was aboard
the
most
fucked up
train of thought

it was the dab
that defied
the conductors calm

with a flick of a switch

I
am
soaking wet
in sweat

TIME IS THE ENEMY

this is what you signed up for

chanted in weak whisper

it is funny

what

you

tell yourself

trying to talk

me

you

down

this evolved

into

a very violent

public

puke sesh

through my two

I was birthing art

the daily digest

had simply decided

it wanted

to see the light

again

and

willed its way

out of me

Matt Barker

it is a scary thing

to lose

touch

with reality

and one

I chose

to face

alone

eyes closed

pulsating

darting

lids

can't contain

this train of thought

was brought

to each

and every

dark corner

between

my two

ears

Black Falcon

I am stained
by your gutsy remains

the cyclical caste
an abated existence

stagnant freight dreams
loom

Shotgun

true fear
will have you
knowing no
logic

I am going to die
in a car

brake lights
instantaneous
unfiltered unreasonable
sheer panic

all too often
I find myself
completely lost
along
this toll free way
to
insanity

when you are drowning
in adrenaline
your mind racing you
down
a one way
full of only
worst case scenarios

I have found

frantically grabbing for the seatbelt
is my
go
to
move

MFA

granite pillars
of emotion
my faithless foundation
shattered
by your
intrinsic infancy

Lackluster Overcompensation

now
it has been
        days
           weeks
              months

since I have produced

            a product
      how
will I
escape
                  at this rate?

shame
      on me…..

24

I write
because
I know
      I will die

     unfortunately
I have begun to see

dear friends
begin to fall
descending into the impenetrably final unconsciousness of
death

without

achieving what had once
fantasized, dreamt, and aspired to be

now

they are gone

TIME IS THE ENEMY

forever
and
all I have left
of them
        is their words................

Déjà Vu

hello
my old friend
as you fall
slowly
towards a grave

of sorts

I wonder

if I will see you

in time

Ode to Brett Billings

My Lover is sad
I ask her what did I do?
Nothing, she says

Well, I thought I could get by on only Loving you

Ha! She cries
Such a noble man
Ya sure that's all?
Didn't have a plan?

Well, I reply
I had quite a few
But none were as good
As only Loving you

Hm... she ponders
With a twinkle in her eye
That is kinda sweet
But u still let me cry

U still made me wait
With no food on my plate

Matt Barker

And I walked around town
With no hope for my fate

Well, u should know
Whenever I did make a plan
I would do just the same
Cuz a plan without you by my side is a plan planned in vain

I been hungry, lonely, and scared,
Sometimes real fukin hi
But I guess I shouldnta complained
Sounds like you were right by my side

Heh, (Ah yes! She giggled)
Yah, I guess you're right
Guess it wasn't so bad
Those walks through the night

But hey man I miss you
Should much like to kiss you
Well, hell, guess I'll have to get by
On only Loving you

Written by Brett Alexander Billings
June 2, 1992 – May 9, 2017
ROAM IN PARADISE

No Mad

chances are
you will
not
be holding
a map
when life
unfolds

Poem to Rant

writers never die
writers never die
inevitable immortality implied in ink
molded by the momentary mindset
has me
recklessly racing
after my fellow
cyclical cynical conductors
who are
ominously off track
aboard
this fucked up train of thought
there will never be enough
people
who are not afraid
to say that
weird fucked up shit
that maybe
hopefully
will get you
to react
have a
unique individual
thought

Bad Habit

in the midst
of a finger flicking picking
fest
I look down
and notice
I have effortlessly acquired
a wild african dogs pelt
by going through
the daily motions
lying motionless
taking shelter
cuticles cannot conceal
the translucent truth
that you are here
for now
don't get comfortable
soon
you will be
picked apart
until
there is nothing left

I am sure
I will see
you again

Peanut Gallery

my world is flat
creatively captured
canvas consistently conceals courage

but

I did not decide
my final form

now

they will not stop

looking

Token

a young
broken heart
takes time
to heal

your soul
poured onto the paper

is now
crumpled
in my hands

86'D

in my restaurant
betrayal
is a dish
served best
cold
face to face

                    we are going out of business

                                      people must like it

                                          some other way

Solid

you are not dumb
but are you

jealous

of the fossils glory
society's sought after cynical showcase
of death

displayed to the masses
remembering what
once was

you are my rock

just one

of many

Ozzy

you stare
smile
fills me
with energy
love
excitement
it is
all relatively
new
for me
for you
I have
a special place
on reserve
for eternity
in my heart

Break

in the crux

of

the rat race

I scurry

out the back door

propped open

by

a roll of trash bags

to an audience

of

trash littered

abandoned alleys

greased city coral

covering

depressed dumpsters

when

I see

a fellow slave

collar glowing

between his lips

Matt Barker

seeking

his few

minutes

of solitude

Competition

you two
dimensional pricks
I know all

of you
will be flat

hiding from the hanging horizontal horizon
unsuccessfully
peering past predetermined protective prisons

in your final frame
you cannot move
you are

                      stuck
                  to the wall

College Conversations

we sit
we talk
you agree
before I
can even
spit
it out

desperation to disprove
intelligence insecurities
raised by the degree

Mentiroso

you long tongue liar
slithery cunt
always
spewing spitting your stories
twisting your truthless tales
in aimless efforts
to conceal
your constant cowardice

I am not worried

karma
will find you
and
fuck you

Reach

an opposed dawn
dampened acceleration
mercifully mists
nefarious nectar
faceless wealth dictates
atop the mislabeled steed
awaiting are
soulless salivating seedlings

                                              for the taking

Accounting

drowned
lifeless
empty words
washed ashore
castaway
I am
as I
watch
my freight dreams
slowly disappear

Bar Back

the working dog
silently watches
through sunken longing

            eyes

as the days
dissolve

time

waits

            for no man

Cigarette Contemplation

my chest is a demon's long bow

pulled

tighter and tighter

cigarette by cigarette

holding it

until

I am weak

then

all hell

will be unleashed

up

on

to

me

Rhetoric

recently
I have been guilty
of leaving
the paper blank

forced production
unavailable

        a writer
        is only
        as good
        as the ink

                that makes it
                onto the paper

you are just the reader

be grateful
for the mental

            stimulation

                      persistence

TIME IS THE ENEMY

                                              killed the cat
                                          and will evolve

                  my deepest dreams
                  into a reality

I write this
before
the words
are confirmed truths

                            like an idiot

                                            I have faith

Light

when the smoke
has cleared
it left
with my sense
of smell
in the process of catching
my cancer quota
one of the five
will be sacrificed

Clockwork

once

red

with passion

before

my eyes

you

are going

out

cold

flaking away

flick

repeat

Felt Pressure

no one cries

for the dying

marker

thoughtlessly bled dry

in front of an unamused impatient audience

only to be

cursed

and thrown away

Polar

    to my fellow swingers
  embrace the emotional erosion
          the

        inherent instinctual isolation
        exposed to the elements
        I question

              my faith
            unity's woven disperse
            functionally frays

                don't trust

                    the rope..........

Typed

raw thoughts captured

in ink

can or cannot

be used

as an assumption

for the rest

who remain

free

but you cannot read

them

Half Full

my tortured stomach
the nefarious puppeteer
in his corruptible body
is recruiting
indiscriminately invading intestines
silently
preaching pained prophecies
I am permanently in
your debt
your gift
to me
inevitable immortality implied in ink
molded by the momentary mindset

                                      something remains….

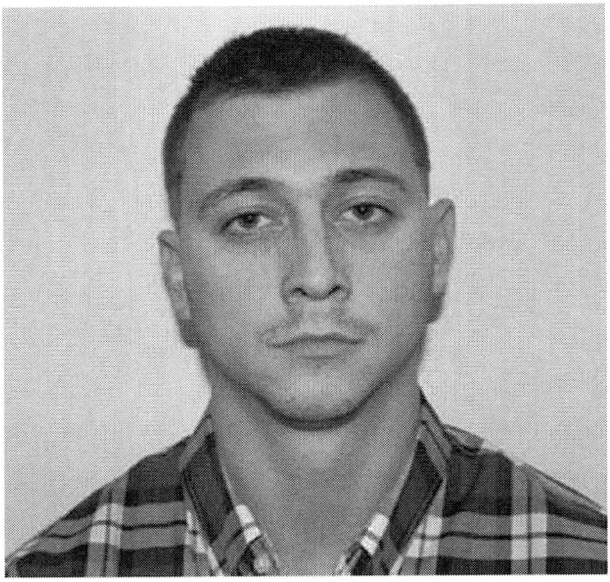

About the Author

Time is the Enemy is Matt Barker's debut book. Barker has been previously published in Adelaide Literary Magazine and was a finalist in the 2018 Adelaide Literary Contest.

Barker grew up in the suburbs of Boston, graduated from Wentworth Institute of Technology, and settled in South Boston. Barker enjoys fishing and riding his moped around the city that shaped him and fostered his lifelong love of the Bruins and Patriots.

Barker's main passion in life is Pembroke Welsh Corgis. Barker believes they radiate an infectious happiness, and plans to breed them in the future.

You can keep up with his work at www.barkerpoetry.com and on Instagram @barkerpoetry

Made in the USA
Middletown, DE
29 August 2019